What Is the Engineering Process?

 HOUGHTON MIFFLIN HARCOURT

Printed in the U.S.A.

ISBN: 978-0-544-07313-5

5 6 7 8 9 10 1083 21 20 19 18 17 16

4500608196   A B C D E F G

Be an Active Reader!

 Look at these words.

tool	engineering
technology	prototype
design	advertisement

 Look for answers to these questions.

How can technology improve products we use every day?

How can technology solve problems?

What is technology?

How can technology make dreams come true?

What is the first step of the design process?

What are the second and third steps of the design process?

What happens during the fourth step of the design process?

What is the fifth step of the design process?

Do all engineers use a design process?

What is a designed system?

What is a technological system?

How can the design process help you?

How do you complete the design process?

How can technology improve products we use every day?

If you were a child about 100 years ago, your milk came in a glass milk bottle. These glass bottles were very heavy and difficult to transport. They could be reused, but they were costly for manufacturers to make.

About 80 years ago, companies started using paper cartons for milk. The paper cartons didn't break, but they were not too strong. Sometimes they leaked. They were lighter and cheaper to produce than glass bottles, though.

Then, around 60 years ago, plastic milk bottles appeared. The plastic bottles were stronger than paper cartons and much lighter than glass. Large bottles could be made with handles, which made pouring easier. Unlike glass, plastic bottles did not break. Today, you can still find milk in all three kinds of containers. Which type of container do you think is best?

glass

paper

plastic

How can technology solve problems?

Do you ever write or draw with a wooden pencil? A pencil is a tool, an object that people use to make, repair, or shape something. A wooden pencil is simply a core of graphite, often called "lead," surrounded by wood. A pencil is a simple and inexpensive tool. However, pencils have to be sharpened. They are thin and can break. They wear down.

To solve this problem, someone invented a mechanical pencil. This pencil is made of metal or plastic. Small sticks of lead inside the pencil can be easily replaced. The mechanical pencil does not break easily, so it can last a long time. It never gets shorter in length because it never has to be sharpened.

When computer touch screens came into use, a different kind of pencil was necessary. Designers made a plastic stylus so that people could write on computer screens.

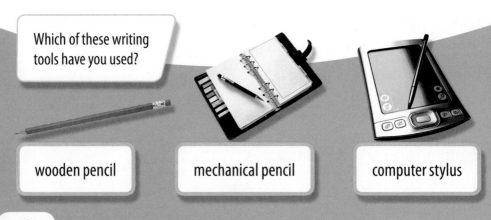

Which of these writing tools have you used?

wooden pencil

mechanical pencil

computer stylus

People use technology every day. How do you use technology?

What is technology?

Changes and improvements to milk containers, pencils, and many other everyday items have come about because of technology. Technology is any designed system, product, or process that people use to solve problems.

Technology gives us ways of imagining new things or improving old ones. People use technology to build better tools and other products. A technology product is something that's designed because it meets a need or desire.

You might think that anything that's "technology" has to run on electricity or have something to do with computers. Not so! In the world around you, there are many more simple technology products, like pencils and milk cartons, than complex ones, like computers and rockets.

5

How can technology make dreams come true?

Have you ever wondered how it feels to fly like a bird? People thought about this for thousands of years.

Around 1488, an artist and inventor named Leonardo da Vinci drew diagrams of flying machines. Since he didn't have the right technology, though, he could not build the machines he designed.

Technology improved. In 1783, people flew the first hot air balloons. In England, in 1849, the first glider flew. Then other inventors in Europe made glider flights. These gliders didn't have engines, so they could not fly very far or go too high. But they were a start. Over time, inventors made improvements. They came closer to making the dream of flight a reality.

German scientist Otto Lilienthal made 2,000 glider flights in the 1890s.

Wilbur and Orville Wright started out as owners of a bicycle shop, but later they became inventors of an engine-powered airplane.

What is the first step of the design process?

During the late 1800s, brothers Wilbur and Orville Wright operated a bicycle shop in Ohio. They read about the glider experiments in Europe. They were fascinated. In 1898, they decided to make and fly an airplane.

The brothers used a design process to make their dream come true. To design means to conceive of something and prepare the plans and drawings for it to be built. A process is a series of steps that occur in a certain order.

The first step in a design process is identifying the problem. The Wright brothers saw that gliders were very limited. They knew they wanted an airplane that a person could control. The airplane needed an engine so that it could fly a long distance.

The Wright brothers built and flew full-size prototypes of their gliders.

What are the second and third steps of the design process?

The second step of the design process is to plan and build. Wilbur and Orville studied and learned more about engineering. Engineering is the application of scientific and mathematical principles to develop something practical. The brothers exchanged ideas with other engineers who were studying flight.

The brothers observed how birds' wings worked. They made a kite to test some of their ideas. They took notes and made drawings to keep track of what worked and what needed to be improved.

The brothers built a wooden prototype glider. A prototype is the original or model on which something is based. If a prototype works, the actual product can be made. If a prototype does not work, it will be improved. Then it will be tested again.

Testing the solution is the third step in the design process. Before they tested their prototype, the Wright brothers did some research to find a place with enough wind for successful flights. They moved to Kitty Hawk, North Carolina.

The first test was a success! Wilbur and Orville improved the prototype. They made more flights and recorded information. They took photographs and studied them.

Although they had some good test flights with the prototype, the brothers knew it needed more work. They moved on to the fourth step in the design process.

This is a detailed drawing of a Wright brothers' aircraft.

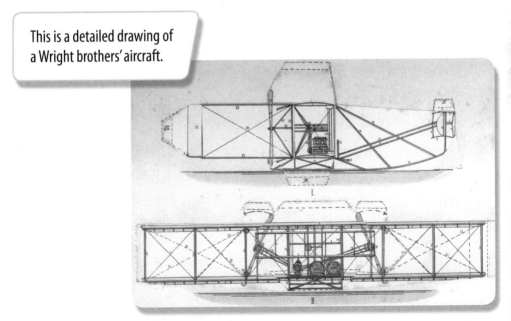

The brothers studied the crashes to see how to improve their prototype glider.

What happens during the fourth step of the design process?

Redesigning the solution is the fourth step in the design process. Wilbur and Orville designed and built a wind tunnel, a building with a specially designed fan that created a strong, straight wind that they could use to test their gliders. They redesigned their prototype, and the new one worked well. They moved their camp a few miles to Kill Devil Hills.

Next, the brothers designed and built an engine and the first aircraft propeller. They added these parts to the glider. They were so sure it would work that they named it the *Flyer*. However, their first few tries were not successful, so they made even more changes.

Then, on December 17, 1903, after 5 years of hard work, the brothers reached their goal. With Orville as the pilot, the *Flyer* flew for twelve seconds. This was the first flight ever for an engine-powered machine that carried a person. The first real airplane was in the air!

One test flight was not enough, so the brothers took turns as pilot and had three more good flights. Each one was a little bit longer than the flight before it.

Only five other people witnessed this historic marvel. Orville asked one of the people to take photographs.

Orville Wright was the first person to fly an engine-powered airplane.

What is the fifth step of the design process?

The fifth and last step in the design process is communicating the results. The same day as their successful test flights, the brothers sent a telegram to their father. It said, in part: "success four flights [T]hursday morning . . . started from Level with engine power alone . . ."

Wilbur and Orville asked their father to tell the newspapers the exciting news. Guess what happened? Some newspapers didn't believe them! No one in the world had been able to fly up until that time. Some people even wondered if the brothers were lying about their accomplishment.

The brothers shared the good news about their successful flights with their father.

THE WESTERN UNION TELEGRAPH COMPANY.

INCORPORATED

23,000 OFFICES IN AMERICA.   CABLE SERVICE TO ALL THE WORLD.

form No. 168.

This Company TRANSMITS and DELIVERS messages only on conditions limiting its liability, which have been amended to by the sender of the following message.
Errors can be guarded against only by repeating a message back to the sending station for comparison, and the Company will not hold itself liable for errors or delays in transmission or delivery of Unrepeated Messages, beyond the amount of tolls paid thereon, nor in any case where the claim is not presented in writing within sixty days after the message is filed with the Company for transmission.
This is an UNREPEATED MESSAGE, and is delivered by request of the sender, under the conditions named above.
ROBERT C. CLOWRY, President and General Manager.

170

RECEIVED at

176 C KA CS 33 Paid.   via Norfolk Va

Kitty Hawk N C Dec 17

Bishop M Wright

7 Hawthorne St

success four flights thursday morning all against twenty one mile wind started from Level with engine power alone average speed through air thirty one miles longest 57 seconds inform Press home Christmas .

Orevelle Wright   525P

The Wrights returned to Ohio, built a new workroom, and made another airplane. They displayed their airplane whenever they could. From 1908 to 1909 they flew over 200 flights in Europe. Finally, the world began to believe the brothers.

In 1914, the Franklin Institute in Philadelphia gave the brothers a medal for their scientific achievements. Sadly, only Orville was alive to receive the award. His brother Wilbur had died two years earlier. When Orville died, he gave the Institute most of his and Wilbur's tools and drawings. These items helped other engineers learn about the Wrights' design process. The Wrights' successes and failures greatly helped the development of safe air travel.

This monument in honor of "First Flight" is on the spot in Kill Devil Hills where Wilbur and Orville made history.

Do all engineers use a design process?

Other engineers were also trying to develop flying machines. These engineers also followed a design process and experienced successes and failures.

A picture of the Wright brothers and their airplane inspired Igor Sikorsky to study airplanes. He also studied Leonardo da Vinci's drawings. Sikorsky thought he could build a helicopter.

When Sikorsky's first few helicopter prototypes failed, he switched to designing airplanes. He was the first to design a plane with more than one engine. He also designed a plane that could take off and land on water.

Sikorsky eventually returned to his ideas about a helicopter. He tested and retested his prototype. In 1940, he flew the first working helicopter in front of a group of amazed reporters.

Igor Sikorsky never gave up on his dream of building a helicopter.

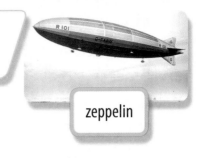

Count Ferdinand von Zeppelin flew the first zeppelin in 1900.

zeppelin

Other pioneers continued to design, test, and build new types of aircraft called airships. Airships such as zeppelins and blimps stayed up in the air because they were filled with gases such as hydrogen or helium. These aircraft were popular until the 1940s. However, after the *Hindenburg* exploded in 1937, airships were seen as unsafe and were no longer used to transport passengers.

flying boat

Flying boats were popular in the 1920s and 1930s. These aircraft flew like planes but landed on the water. They were heavy and expensive to use, so other types of aircraft replaced them, eventually resulting in the seaplane.

Tin Goose

Most airplanes were made of wood or wood and metal. In 1927, engineers at the Ford Motor Company made the first all-metal airplane. They called it the *Tin Goose*! Engineers continued to design better and safer all-metal airplanes.

What is a designed system?

A designed system consists of all the tools, parts, and processes that work together to achieve a goal. A transportation system, such as a city's bus system, is a designed system. Airplanes are used in a designed system that helps us transport people and goods all over the world. The designed system for airlines includes airplanes and airports. The terminals, runways, parking lots, and service trucks are all part of the designed system. Air traffic lanes in the sky let the pilots fly safely from place to place. Radar shows where airplanes are located. Computers keep track of schedules, passengers, and cargo. One of the biggest parts of the system is people!

This designed system helps transport people and goods all over the world.

A designed system is part of your designed world—the aspects of your life that are designed and built by people, such as energy systems, highways, parks, and buildings.

Look at this chart to find out more about the parts of a designed system for airplane transportation.

Parts of a Designed System

Part	Example : Airplane Transportation System
Goal—what the system aims to do	to move cargo and passengers safely through the air from place to place
Input—what is put into the system to meet the goal	fuel for the airplane; cargo; people to ride the airplane; pilots to fly the airplane; flight attendants on the plane to take care of passengers; people on the ground to help the airplane
Processes—describe means by which the goal is to be achieved	airports, air traffic lanes, departure and arrival schedules
Output—the end product	safe and timely delivery of people and cargo
Feedback—information that tells whether or not the output is successful	records of when airplanes left and arrived

What is a technological system?

An airplane is a good example of a technological system. A technological system is a group of tools, parts, and processes that use technology to work together.

Look at the outside of an airplane. You see the body, wings, and landing gear. The rudder is a wing at the back of the plane that helps control the plane's direction. Large airplanes have several huge jet engines. Smaller airplanes may have one or more propellers. Floatplanes have ski-like floats as part of the landing gear.

Inside, the airplane is full of electronic equipment. Pilots talk to the ground crew by radio. Computer instruments show the plane's location and speed as well as the weather.

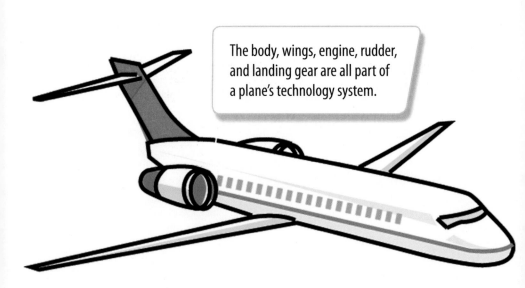

The body, wings, engine, rudder, and landing gear are all part of a plane's technology system.

Heating, air conditioning, and lighting systems keep the airplane comfortable. The bathrooms have chemical toilets. Many planes have kitchens where flight attendants make coffee or heat up meals. On some airplanes, you can watch movies, play video games, or listen to music. All of these things are part of an airplane's technological system.

All of the parts of a technological system were made possible by technology processes. A technology process is a series of steps used in the making of a product or the achievement of a technological goal. You're using a technology process when you follow a recipe or use a remote control to set up a streaming video on your TV.

The pilot uses flight instruments to fly the plane in the right direction and at the correct speed.

How can the design process help you?

Now that you understand how the design process works, you can use it yourself. You might be surprised at how many chances you'll have in your life to use the design process. You can use it to test things as well as make things.

Imagine that you are at a toy store looking for a new model glider airplane for your collection. A company's advertisement for one glider claims it's the fastest of all the model gliders on the market. You are not sure the claim is true, but you buy the glider. At home, you use the design process to test the claim.

Step 1: You identify the problem. You need to find out if the new glider really is the fastest toy glider available.

The design process can help you figure out if an advertisement is telling the truth about a product.

Step 2: You plan and build. Your problem is that you need to see if the advertising claim was true. Your solution will be to design a test that shows whether the glider really is faster than other gliders. How you do it? Design and build a test runway. Measure a section of a large, bare floor or an outdoor space. Put tape at the starting and finishing lines.

Step 3: You test the glider. Fly it and check how many seconds it takes to reach the finish line. Write the time on a chart. Then fly all of the other gliders the same way and record their times, too.

Glider	Time of Flight (in seconds)	Observation
Blue	13	second
Green	16	fourth
Black	15	third
New	11	fastest

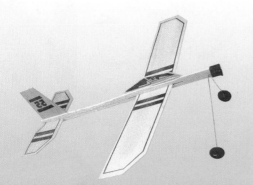

You have to fly each glider in exactly the same way to have an accurate test.

How do you complete the design process?

Step 4: If your first test was well designed, you don't have to redesign anything. Don't be discouraged, though, if your test didn't work. Design engineers understand the meaning of the saying "If at first you don't succeed, try, try again."

Step 5: You communicate your results. The new glider really is the fastest. Send an email to the toy company describing your design process, or let your friends know through a text message or email.

Now that you know how well the design process works, look for more opportunities to use it!

Design engineers must learn from failure and start over again.

Improve a Design

Can you find some piece of technology in your daily life that you could improve? Could you design a better toothbrush or ice-cream scoop? Brainstorm some ideas and choose one. Identify the problem. Plan and build a prototype by drawing your ideas on paper. Get feedback from classmates, family, or friends. Use the new ideas you get to create new drawings that improve on the design. Finally, draw a labeled picture of your finished product. This is your prototype. Explain why it is an improvement on an existing product.

Write a Report

Use the Internet and library resources to learn about someone who used the design process to invent or improve something. Remember that the invention doesn't have to be a complicated technology. Write a report with an introduction and a conclusion explaining how the person used the steps of the design process.

Glossary

advertisement [ad·ver·tiz·muhnt] A public notice or announcement of information designed to communicate a message to a viewer or listener about a product or service.

design [dih·ZYN] To conceive something and prepare the plans and drawings for it to be built.

engineering [en·juh·NIR·ing] The application of scientific and mathematical principles to develop something practical.

prototype [PROH·tuh·typ] The original or model on which something is based.

technology [tek·NOL·uh·jee] Any designed system, product, or process used to solve problems.

tool [TOOL] Anything used to help people shape, build, or produce things to meet their needs.